und Andere, A. G. Herzberg

Music Album for the Piano

und Andere, A. G. Herzberg

Music Album for the Piano

ISBN/EAN: 9783744793001

Printed in Europe, USA, Canada, Australia, Japan

Cover: Foto ©Thomas Meinert / pixelio.de

More available books at **www.hansebooks.com**

MUSIC ALBUM

FOR THE PIANO.

INDEX

* Used by permission of Oliver Ditson & Co.

JULES BERR,

EDITOR AND PUBLISHER.

LOAO, the Printer, Sansom St. Hall.

Hoofland's German Bitters
AND
HOOFLAND'S GERMAN TONIC

Prepared by Dr. C. M. JACKSON, Philadelphia, Pa.

The Great Remedies for all Diseases
OF THE
LIVER, STOMACH OR DIGESTIVE ORGANS.

HOOFLAND'S GERMAN BITTERS

Is composed of the pure juices (or, as they are medicinally termed, *Extracts*) of Roots, Herbs and Barks, making a preparation highly concentrated, and entirely *free from Alcoholic admixture of any kind.*

HOOFLAND'S GERMAN TONIC

Is a combination of all the ingredients of the Bitters, with the purest quality of *Santa Cruz Rum*, Orange, etc., making one of the most pleasant and agreeable remedies ever offered to the public.

Those preferring a Medicine free from Alcoholic admixture, will use

HOOFLAND'S GERMAN BITTERS.

In cases of nervous depression, when some alcoholic stimulus is necessary,

HOOFLAND'S GERMAN TONIC

should be used. The Bitters or the Tonic are both equally good, and contain the same medicinal virtues.

CAUTION.

Hoofland's German remedies are counterfeited. See that the signature of C. M. JACKSON is on the wrapper of each bottle. All others are counterfeit.

Principal Office and Manufactory at the German Medicine Store,

No. 631 Arch Street, Philadelphia,

CHARLES M. EVANS,

German Druggist, Proprietor, Formerly C. M. & Jackson & Co.

FOR SALE BY ALL DRUGGISTS AND DEALERS IN MEDICINES.

PRICES.

Hoofland's German Bitters, per bottle,	$1.00
" " " half dozen,	5.00
Hoofland's German Tonic, per bottle,	1.50
or a half dozen for	7.50

Do not forget to examine well the article you buy, in order to get the genuine.

The Tonic is put up in quart bottles.

LOAG, THE PRINTER, SANSOM ST. HALL.

1

Dedié à Mad'lle Kate Longstreth.

Minnehaha

POLKA

For the Piano Forte.

Composed by A. G. HERZBERG.

Published by JULES BERR.

Entered according to Act of Congress, in the year 1868, by JULES BERR, in the Clerk's Office of the District Court for the Eastern District of Pennsylvania.

IGNATIUS LUTZ,

Cabinet & Upholstering

WAREROOMS,

No. 121 South Eleventh St.

IMPORTER AND DEALER IN

FINE FURNITURE,

PATENTED RECLINING CHAIR,

Superior to any in the Country.

MANUFACTURED AND

SOLD ONLY IN MY ESTABLISHMENT.

LOAG, PRINTER, PHILADELPHIA.

MINNIÉ POLKA.

By HERZBERG.

Published by Jules Barr.

1

LACEY, MEEKER & CO.

Manufacturers and Importers of

AND

WHOLESALE AND RETAIL

DEALERS IN

SADDLERY ᴬᴺᴰ HARNESS

Harness from $14.00 to $500.00 per Set,

No. 1216 Chestnut St.

PHILADELPHIA.

New York House, 27 Chambers St.

LDAG, PRINTER, PHILADELPHIA.

Published by Jules Barr.

For dancing Polka.
Da Capo. *Coda.*

Published by Jales Barr.

3

EVENING TELEGRAPH

Published every Afternoon, except Sundays,

AT

108 South Third St.

PHILADELPHIA,

Has the largest circulation of any Evening Paper in the United States, contains all the News of the Associated Press and the European and United States Telegraph Co., up to 5 o'clock P. M., with special reports from Washington and every leading News Centre, North and South.

THE EVENING TELEGRAPH

Also contains the Leading Editorials from the New York Herald, Tribune, Times, World and the most prominent and influential Newspapers throughout the United States. Its original matter consisting of Editorials, Local News, Reports, Markets, Financial Reports, Stock Reports, is interesting and reliable. In every Saturday's Edition is published

An Original Illustrated Humorous Article on Local Subjects, entitled

"Our Saturday Night Supper Table Series."

Another Leading Feature of

THE EVENING TELEGRAPH

Consists of lavish and copious Literary Articles selected from the Leading English Monthlies and Periodicals, such as "Temple Bar," "Cornhill Magazine," "All the Year Round," "Once a Week," "St James' London Society," "Leisure Hours," and "Belgravia."

To Advertisers:

The circulation of the Evening Telegraph, besides being greater than any other Evening Paper in Philadelphia, extends to all the Towns and Cities adjacent to the City. It is, therefore, the most desirable medium of Advertising for Business Men. Real Estate owners, &c.

Its advertising rates are lower, in proportion to its circulation, than any other Paper published. Address,

CHAS. E. WARBURTON,

Publisher.

Published by Jules Burr.

HANNIG, SCHEIBE, MEYER & HERZBERG

CONSTITUTE THE

UNION

PIANO MANUF'G CO.

They manufacture at their two Factories in this city, and sell at their Warerooms,

1017 Walnut Street,

Their Beautiful Patent Improved

AGRAFFE BRIDGE PIANOS,

Which, in quality of tone and beautiful workmanship, surpass all so called Agraffe and other style Pianos.

SOLD AT VERY REASONABLE PRICES,

And fully guaranteed for seven years. It will be to your interest to give the above Company a call before purchasing elsewhere.

G. HERZBERG, Sec'y,

1017 Walnut Street.

LLOYD, THE PRINTER, SANSOM ST. HALL.

IDYLLE

Pour le

PIANO

PAR

Charles B. Lysberg.

Published by JULES BERR.

IDYLLE.

CHAS. B. LYSBERG.

Published by Jules Berr.

Published by Jules Benr.

Published by Jules Burr.

Published by Jules Barr.

Ped.
cres.
Ped.
rall.
Ped.
cres.
Ped.
Ped.
con moto e passione.
rit.
Ped.
p
poco a poco.
Ped.
più piano e ritard.
pp
Fine.
Ped.

CONSOLATION.

SONGS WITHOUT WORDS. No. 9. MENDELSSOHN.

PIANO.

10

WM. P. CAMPBELL,

IMPORTER AND MANUFACTURER

OF

Cloaks,

CLOAK TRIMMINGS,

AND

Furs,

1124 Chestnut Street,

PHILADELPHIA.

AOAO, THE PRINTER, RANSOM ST. HALL.

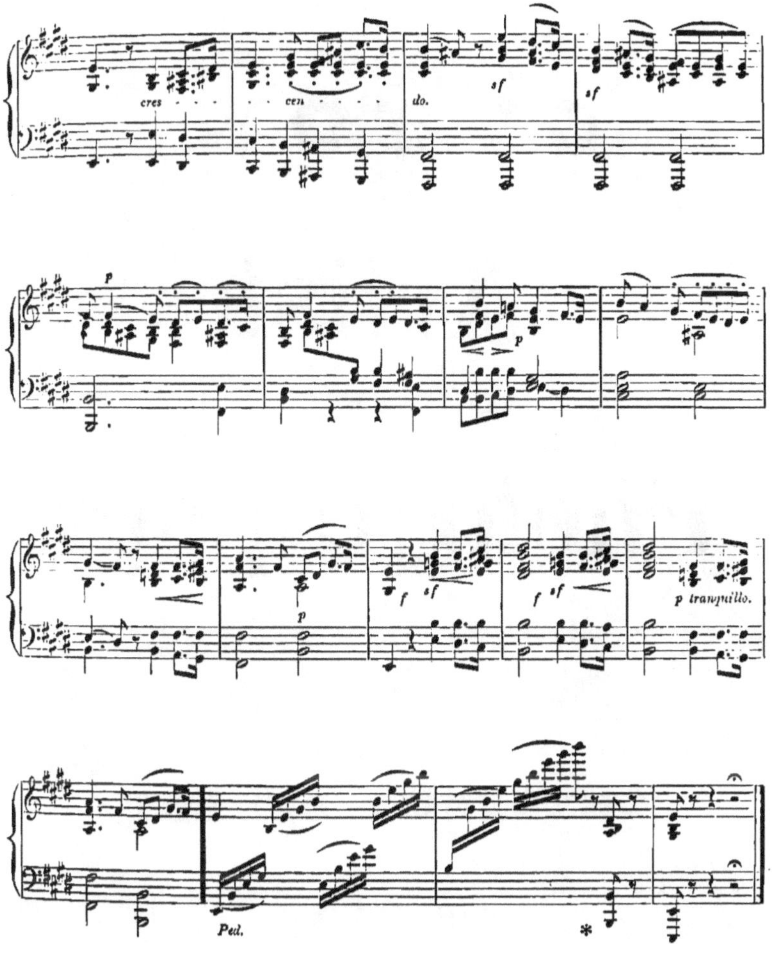
cres - - - - - cen - - - - - do.
sf
p
f
p tranquillo.
Ped.
*

GIHON,

Artist

AND

Photographer

1024

CHESTNUT STREET,

PHILADELPHIA.

GRAND

TRIUMPHAL

MARCH

Composed for the Piano Forte,

BY

J. CONCONE.

Published by JULES BERR.

MARCHE TRIOMPHALE.

J. C. CONCONE.

Published by Jules Barr.

Published by Jules Burn.

Mrs. M. A. Binder,

IMPORTER OF

DRESS & CLOAK TRIMMINGS,

In every variety and style, for each Season; also,

PARIS FASHIONS IN

PAPER PATTERNS,

For Ladies' and Children's Dress.

WEDDING, TRAVELING & MOURNING DRESSES

OR SUITS,

Made to order in 24 Hours, in the most Elegant Manner.

Hoop Skirts, French Corsets,

Jet, Gilt and Pearl Bands for the Hair, &c.

FANCY GOODS OF EVERY KIND.

Sets of Patterns for Merchants & Dress Makers,

NOW READY.

No. 1031 Chestnut Street,

PHILADELPHIA.

Published by Jules Burr.

E. J. WILLIAMS.   B. J. WOODWARD.

WILLIAMS & WOODWARD,

PROPRIETORS OF

"THE MURPHEY"

House Furnishing

STORE.

English and American   English and American

CUTLERY.   TEA TRAYS.

CHILDRENS' CARRIAGES, &c.

922 (NINE TWENTY-TWO) Chestnut St.

PHILADELPHIA.

Steam and Packet Ships, Hotels and Boarding Houses fitted out with every
requisite article for Kitchen and Pantry use, at short notice.

LOAG, THE PRINTERS, SANSOM ST. HALL.

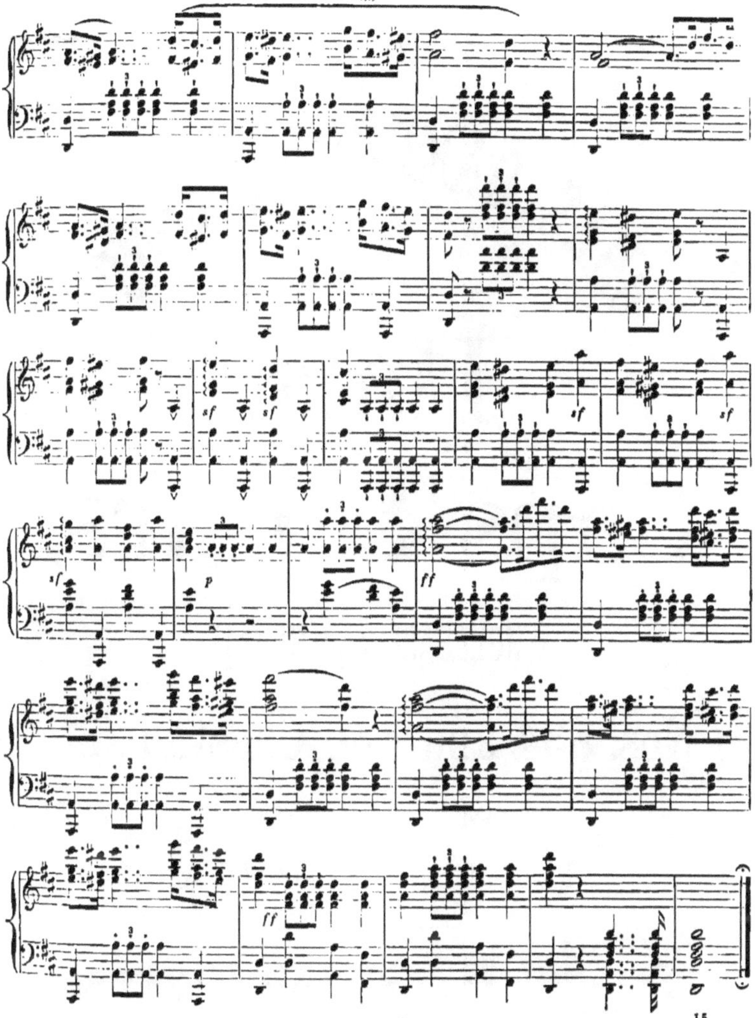
sf
sf
sf
sf
sf
p
ff
ff

CHAS. OAKFORD & SONS,

Importers & Manufacturers of

Hats,
Caps & Furs,

WHOLESALE and RETAIL,

Nos. 834 and 836 Chestnut St.

CONTINENTAL HOTEL,

PHILADELPHIA.

Latest European Styles.

GRANDE DUCHESSE DE GEROLSTEIN

WALTZ

For the Piano Forte.

BY

OFFENBACH.

Published by JULES BERR.

LOAG, THE PRINTER, SANSOM ST. HALL.

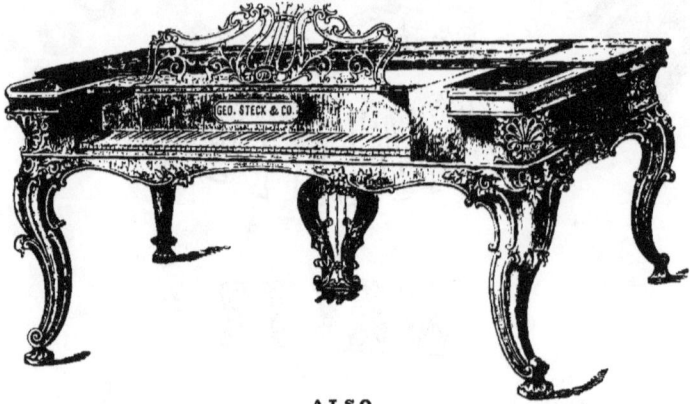

LA GRANDE DUCHESSE DE GEROLSTEIN.

GRANDE VALSE.

OPERA BOUFFE de
J. OFFENBACH.

Published by Jules Borr.

Magazin des Modes.

SPECIALTIES IN

LADIES'

Cloaks,
Mantillas,

BLACK DRESS SILKS,

LACE SHAWLS.

LADIES' DRESS FURS, &c., &c.

J. W. PROCTOR & CO.

920 Chestnut Street,

PHILADELPHIA.

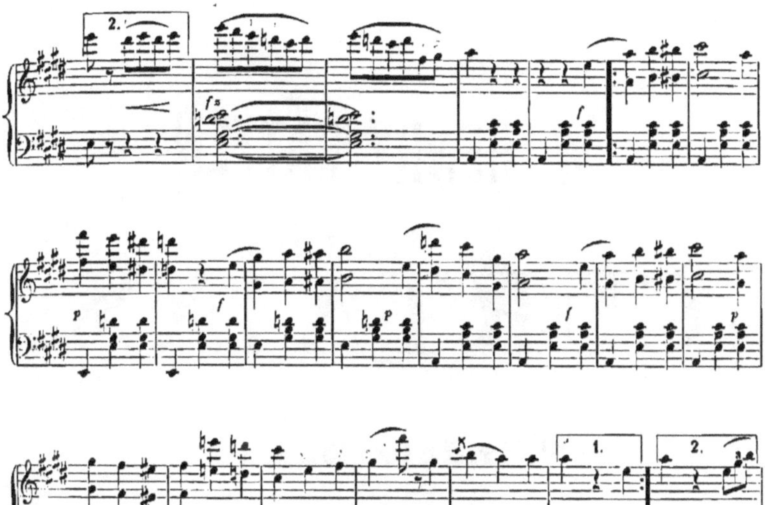
2.
1.
2.

W. HENRY PATTEN,

CURTAINS,

Window Shades,

VERANDAH AWNINGS, BEDDING,

And General Upholstery,

1408 Chestnut Street,

PHILADELPHIA.

LOAG, THE PRINTER, SANSOM ST. HALL.

Published by Jules Berr.

JAMES T. BLACK.   R. J. M. WHITESIDE.

THOMPSON BLACK'S SON & CO.

Broad and Chestnut Streets,

PHILADELPHIA,

DEALERS IN

Fine Teas & Coffees

Choice Brands of

FAMILY FLOUR,

HERMETICALLY SEALED

FRUITS & VEGETABLES,

Imported and Domestic

PICKLES AND PRESERVES,

And every variety of

CHOICE FAMILY GROCERIES.

Orders by Mail will receive prompt attention.

IOAG, THE PRINTER, FARSON ST HALL.

Published by Jules Herr.

19

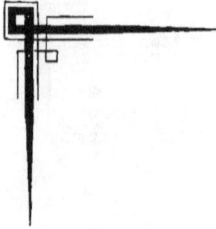

J. W. SCOTT & CO.

Fine Shirts,

AND

PARIS AND LONDON NOVELTIES

In Gentlemen's Wear,

N^{O.} 814 CHESTNUT STREET,

PHILADELPHIA.

ALL ORDERS PROMPTLY ATTENDED TO.

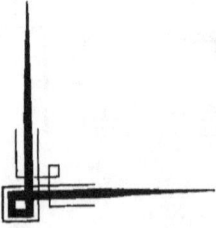

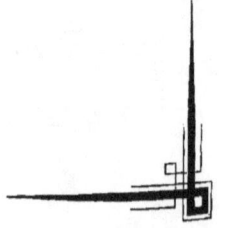

LOAG THE PRINTER, SANSOM ST. HALL

MABEL WALTZES.

D. GODFREY.

N°. 1.   CORNET SOLO.

WALTZ.   p dol.

20

Published by Jules Berr.

46

PHILADELPHIA

Evening Bulletin,

A DAILY AFTERNOON PAPER,

Published at the

NEW BULLETIN BUILDING,

No. 607 Chestnut Street,

PHILADELPHIA.

Contains the Latest News by Telegraph and the Mails to the moment of going to Press; Local Reports, Markets, Finance, Literary Matter, Foreign and Domestic Correspondence, Editorial Comments on Current Events, &c., &c., &c.

Served to Subscribers in the City at Eighteen Cents per Week, payable to the Carrier; or by Mail at Eight Dollars per annum, in advance.

GIBSON PEACOCK,   **F. L. FETHERSTON,**
Editor.   *Publisher.*

LOAG, THE PRINTER, SANSOM ST HALL.

Waltz D.C.

N°. 2.

2d time 8va.......

Fine.

Published by Jules Berr.

"The Perfection of Mechanism."

WILLCOX & GIBBS'

CELEBRATED

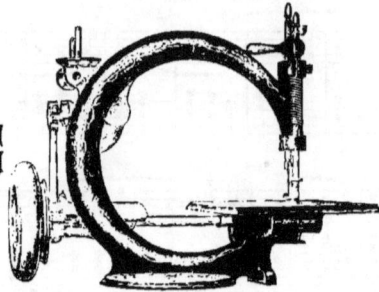

Letter G   Silent

FAMILY

SEWING MACHINES

No. 720 Chestnut Street,

PHILADELPHIA.

KING, THE PRINTER, SANSOM ST. HALL

Dédié à Ma Nièce Berthe Tribourg.

ROMEO AND JULIETTE

Gounod's Opera.

FANTASIE AIR,

Arranged by H. A. Clarke.

Published by JULES BERR.

FANTASIE ON AIRS

FROM

ROMÉO et JULIETTE.

Arr. by H. A. CLARKE.

52

CLOTHING

MADE WITH

CARE AND ELEGANCE,

SUITABLE FOR THE

WARDROBE OF ANY GENTLEMAN.

WANAMAKER & BROWN,

THE "OAK HALL" BUILDING,

Sixth St., from Market to Minor,

PHILADELPHIA.

DAV. THE PRINTER, SANSOM ST. HALL

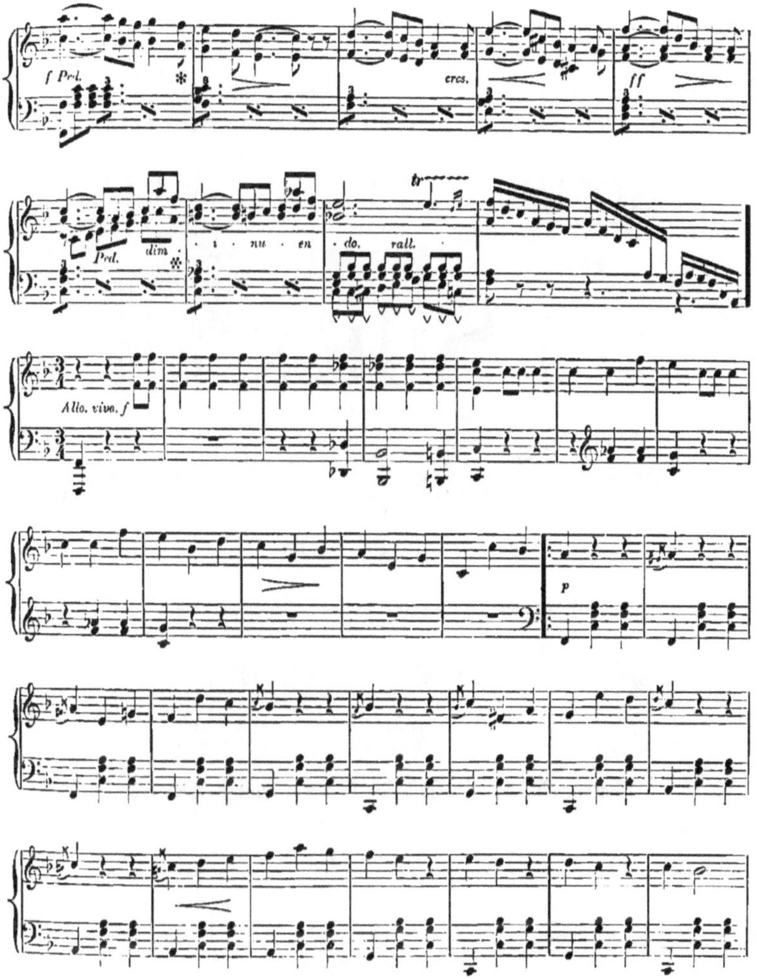
f Ped.
cres.
ff
Ped.
dim.
tr
· i nu · en do. rall.
Allo. vivo. f
p

HOMER COLLADAY & CO.

IMPORTERS OF

Silks

Dress Goods, Cloaks, Shawls,

&c.

A Choice Assortment constantly on hand, embracing the choicest

PARISIAN NOVELTIES,

WHOLESALE AND RETAIL,

Nos. 818 & 820 Chestnut Street,

PHILADELPHIA.

LOAG, THE PRINTER, SANSOM ST. HALL.

Published by Jules Berr.

FAUST GOUNOD'S OPERE.

LE PARLATE D'AMOR.

IN THE LANGUAGE OF LOVE.

BEAUTIES OF FAUST.   GOUNOD.

Allegretto Agitato.

p

cres.

dim.

SIEBEL.

Le par-la-te d'a - mor,   O cu - - - - ri   fior,   Di - te - le che l'a-
In the language of love,   O gen - - - - tle flower,   Say to her I   a -

- do - - ro,   Ch'e il solo mio te - so - ro,   Di - te - le che il mio cor . . . . .
- dore her,   Say she's my love my trea - sure,   Say that she of   my   heart,   of   my

cres.

Published by Jules Berr.

25

WHEELER & WILSON'S

LOCK-STITCH

Sewing Machines

RECEIVED THE ONLY

GOLD MEDAL,

PARIS EXPOSITION, 1867.

PHILADELPHIA SALESROOMS

No. 704 CHESTNUT STREET,

PETERSON & LITTLE, Ag'ts.

LOAG, THE PRINTER, SANSOM ST. HALL.

58

Lan - gue d'a-mor . . . . Le par-la-te d'a - mor, O ca - - - ri
life is the joy, ... And assure her my love is strong and

fior, . . Recate i miei sos-pi - - ri, Narrate i miei mar-ti - - ri,
pure, . . Tell her my hopes and fears, Tell her her presence en - dears, . .

pp

cres cen

Ditele, o ca - ri fior, . . Quel ch'ho . . nel cor. . . .
Ev-'ry bright hour for me, . . So speak, . . sweet flowers. . .

do. dim. p cres.

Recitative.

Son viz - zi, a - himè! lo stregon ma-le-
What, fa - ded! ah, me! thus the bold, evil

dim.

f

26

Published by Jules Berr.

Tempo primo.

- det - to mal di-ceva or   or.
soro'-rer foretold at the   fair.

cres.

Recit.   **Andante.**

Non po-trai   più   sen-za che   mo - ra   Toc - ca - re un   fior.
I may not   touch   a blooming   flow - er, but it   shall   wither.

p

Andante. (♩ = 56.)

Se ba-gnas-si la man nell'acqua   san - ta?   Vien là   quando il dì muor?
But my hand in ho-ly wa-ter I   bathe.   See now   will they wither?

pp

A pre-gar   Mar-ghe - ri - ta   Ed ora ve-di-am!   vediam presto!   Sono appas-
Here to pray   cometh dai - ly   the sweet gentle maid,   Once more venture,—   now are they

p   *p*   *p*

Wm. D. Rogers,

COACH

AND

Light Carriage

BUILDER,

MANUFACTURER OF

FIRST-CLASS CARRIAGES

ONLY,

1009 & 1011 Chestnut St,

PHILADELPHIA.

1040, THE PRINTER, SANSOM ST. HALL.

Tempo 1º. Allegretto,

si - ti?   No!   Sa - tan   sci vin-to   già.
faded?   no!   Sa - tan!   thy spell hath   failed.

pp cres. molto.

In   lor   sol - tan - - - to ho   fò;   Parlin per   me!   Da lor le sia sve-
Thus   ev - er   frand   must fail;   Speak then for me!   Tell her, sweet flowers, I

staccato.

- la - - to   Il mi-se-ro mio sta - to   El-la pe-nar   mi   fà . . . . E an-
love   her,   Bright are the heavens a-bove   her,   Bright is the earth   for   me, ... the

cor . . . nol sa,   In ques-ti fio-ri ho   fò . . . . Par - lin   per
earth, . .   for me,   When her loved form I   see . . . . Speak,   then   for

Published by Jules Ber.

H. & A. C. VAN BEIL,

WINE MERCHANTS,

For Families and the Trade.

Importers of the Finest Brands of

Champagnes, Sherry, Port & Madeira Wines, Brandies, &c.

Very Fine Old Rye Whiskies.

H. & A. C. VAN BEIL,

1310 Chestnut St,

Nearly opposite the Mint,

PHILADELPHIA.

LOAG, THE PRINTER, SANSOM ST. HALL

me. . . .   Se non ar - dis - ce a - mo - re,   Possa in sua voce il fio - - re,
me. . . .   What yet I never have told   her,   Say that my arms would enfold   her,

Sve-la - re del   mio cor . . . . . . Tut - - to   l'ar - dor, . .   l'ar -
Guarding from ev - 'ry ill . . . . . . Lov - - ing her still, . .   Thus

- dor,   tut - - to   l'ar - dor,   l'ar - dor, tut - - to   l'ar-
speak,   sweet   flowers, for   me,   Thus plead, sweet   flowers, for

dor.
me. . .

Les Fifres

DE LA GARDE

Polka Militaire.

PAR

J. ASCHER.

Published by JULES BERR.

J. T. DELACROIX,

Importer and Dealer in

Carpetings

Of all Descriptions,

Mattings, Oil Cloths, Rugs,

&c., &c.

WHOLESALE AND RETAIL,

Warehouse, 37 South Second Street,

ABOVE CHESTNUT STREET,

PHILADELPHIA.

LOAG, THE PRINTER, SANSOM ST. HALL.

LES FIFRES DE LA GARDE.

2me. POLKA MILITAIRE.

J. ASCHER.

Published by Jules Borr.

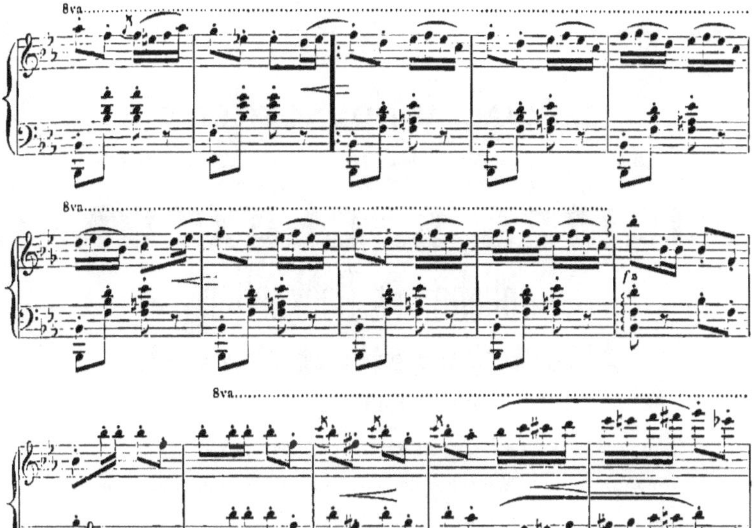
8va
8va
8va
fz
8va
8va
1.
2.

TRIO.

Published by Jules Burr.

$22. $22.

NOVELTY

Sewing Machine

UNEQUALLED IN

EXCELLENCE AND DURABILITY,

WILL HEM, BRAID & EMBROIDER

In the best manner; and also

DO ALL KINDS OF FAMILY SEWING,

Equal to any others in the market.   *Before purchasing elsewhere call at*

EMMES, CRAM & CO.

Agents for Pennsylvania,

922 Chestnut St., Philadelphia.

This Machine is complete with Table for 22 Dollars.

Published by Jules Borr.

33

74

H. TIREL,

Successor to **A. S. MARY AINE,**

Patented January 5th, 1858.

FRENCH STEAM

Dyeing

A N D

SCOURING ESTABLISHMENT.

All kinds of Ladies' and Gentlemen's garments Dyed and Cleaned in a superior manner.

PIECE WORK DONE AT A SHORT NOTICE.

No. 210 South Eighth Street,

PHILADELPHIA.

LOAG, THE PRINTER, SANSOM ST. HALL

Published by Jules Bern.

John L. Gihon,

Artist,

AND

PHOTOGRAPHER,

No. 1024 Chestnut Street,

PHILADELPHIA.

Mr. Gihon desires to direct attention to the fact that his combined professions enable him to impart to all of his productions an unusual degree of pictorial excellence. All of the work executed at his establishment is finished under his own immediate surveillance.

The success that has thus far attended his labors, and the satisfaction expressed by his patrons, lead him to hope for a continuation of the same generous support.

GIHON,

Artist and Photographer,

No. 1024 Chestnut Street,

PHILADELPHIA.

LOAG, THE PRINTER, SANSOM ST HALL.

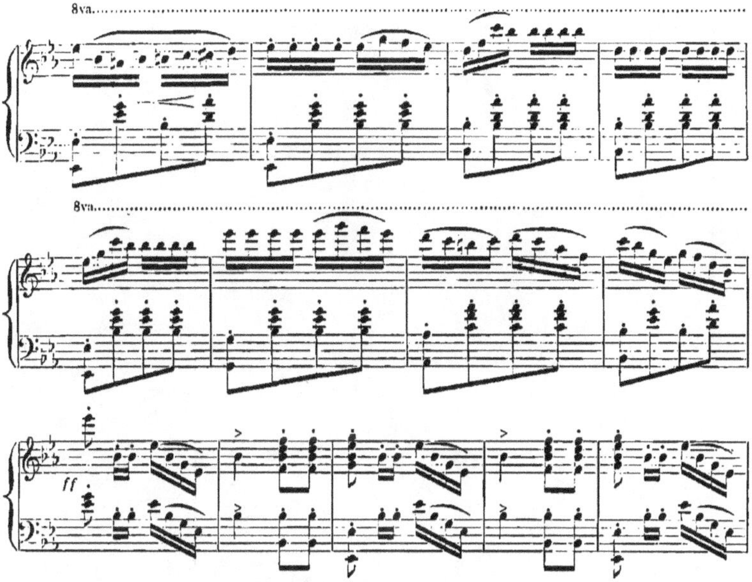
8va
8va
ff
8va
ff
p
8va
ff
fff
trem.

78

SOUVENIR.

St. Lawrence Hall,
Great St. James Street, Montreal,
H. Hogan, Proprietor.

The only first-class Hotel in Montreal.

NOTICE BY THE EDITOR.

In remembrance of this Hotel, I take the liberty of recommending, not the House, which is known the world over, but the Proprietor, H. HOGAN, Esq., as a most perfect gentleman, and I beg him to accept this slight tribute as an expression of my gratitude.

JULES BERR.

PERLE D'ALLEMAGNE.

BLUETTE À LA MAZURKA.

J. ASCHER.

Published by Jules Borr.

PARLOR JEWELRY STORE.

W. B. ELTONHEAD,

GOLD

AND

Silversmith,

1322 CHESTNUT STREET,

PHILADELPHIA.

IMPORTER AND DEALER IN

DIAMONDS, CORAL, STONE CAMEOS,

And all kinds of Precious Stones.

Having adapted my Establishment to Manufacturing, I am now prepared to make
to order, all the most unique and intricate designs in Gold and Silver,
entirely different from anything now offered for sale in
this Country.

IMPORTER OF ALL THE

CELEBRATED EUROPEAN WATCHES

AMERICAN WATCHES

Direct from the Manufacturers.

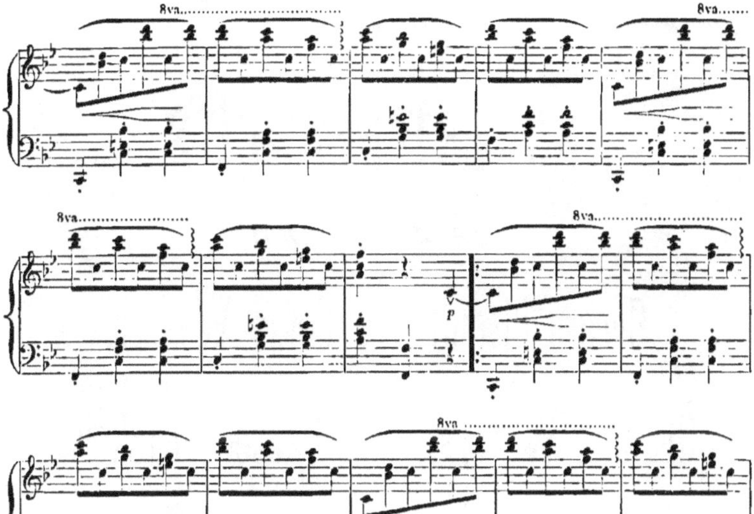
8va
8va
8va
8va
8va
p
f
p

ROBERT PEARCE'S

CELEBRATED

Cream Biscuit,   Pearl Wafers,

Graham Wafers,   Butter Crackers,

Wine Biscuit, Soda Biscuit,

GRAHAM CRACKERS,

OYSTER CRACKERS,

WATER CRACKERS.

For Sale by all first-class Grocers.

Published by John Barr.

R. HOSKINS & CO.

STATIONERS,

ENGRAVERS,

Envelope and Blank Book Manufacturers

AND

PRINTERS,

No. 913 Arch Street, Philadelphia.

Novelties in Wedding Cards.

Monograms and Initials Stamped on Paper and Envelopes, in Colors, free of Charge.

LOAG, THE PRINTER, FANTOM ST. HALL.

85

SINGER'S

New Family

SEWING MACHINE

Is Simple, Durable, Quiet and Light-running,

And capable of performing an astonishing range and variety of work.

Will Hem, Fell, Stitch, Braid, Gather, Cord, Tuck,
Quilt, Embroider, &c.

OFFICE REMOVED TO

No. 1106 Chestnut Street,

PHILADELPHIA.

The Singer Manufacturing Co.

WM. E. COOPER, Agent.

40 Published by Jules Berr.

MARCHE

DU

(CORONATION.)

MEYERBEER

Published by JULES BERR.

McKEONE, VAN HAAGEN & CO.

MANUFACTURERS OF

AMERICAN COMPANY

Honey, Glycerine, Palm, Elder Flower, Boquet,

And over 100 other different kinds of

HIGHLY PERFUMED

FANCY TOILET SOAPS,

Warranted equal to English or French, and 50 per cent. cheaper.
For sale by all Druggists and Dealers in Fine Soaps,
and Wholesale only at

No. 32 South Front Street, Philadelphia.

No. 30 Barclay Street, New York.

LOAG, THE PRINTER, SANSOM St. HALL.

MARCHE DU SACRE.

G. MEYERBEER.

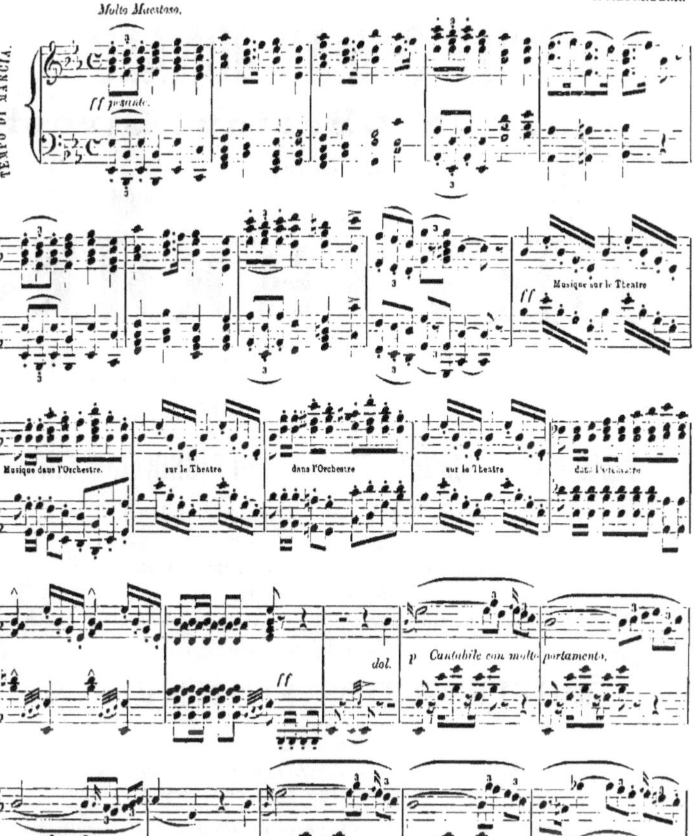

KULP & MAC DONALD,

No. 1206 Chestnut Street,

PHILADELPHIA,

Invite the attention of the public to their large and varied stock of Staple and Housefurnishing

DRY GOODS

COMPRISING

French, Barnsley, and Irish Damask Table Linens,
Barnsley Sheetings, all qualities and widths.

PILLOW CASE LINENS, RICHARDSON'S SHIRTING LINENS,

German, French and Barnsley Damask and Huck Towels,
"   "   " Napkins and Doylies,
Embroidered Piano and Table Covers,
Marseilles Quilts,
All varieties of Sheeting and Shirting Muslins. Complete Stock of
Carefully Selected

WHITE GOODS, FLANNELS, &c.

[CARD.]

The long connection of Mr. Kulp with the old and valued firm of J. V. Cowell & Son, emboldens him to hope for a share of the patronage so liberally extended to that deserving house, and he trusts that by still increased attention to the wants of their customers the new firm may establish a reputation second to none in their line of business.

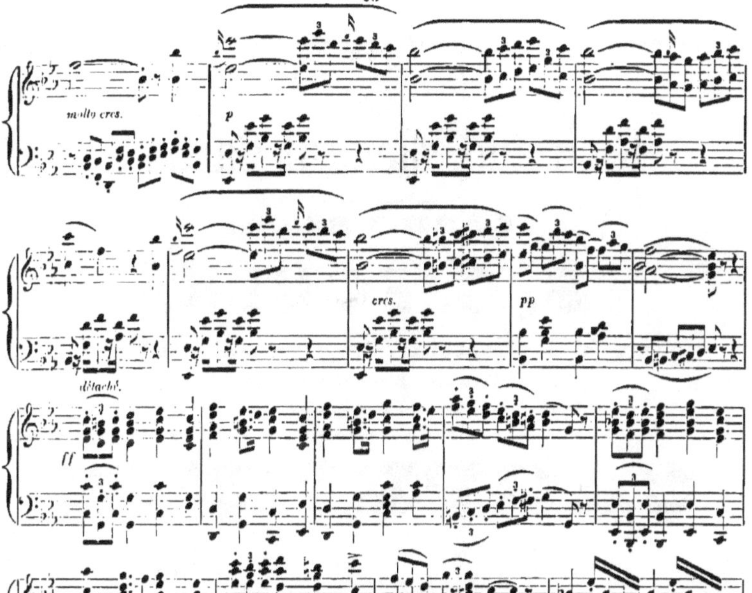

Published by Jules Beer.

Rich and Elegant Carpets.

CASH TRADE.

S. C. FOULK,

No. 25 South Second Street,

Corner of Black Horse Alley,

Respectfully invites the attention of the Public to his extensive and elegant assortment of

CARPETINGS

Floor Oil Cloths, Window Shades,

&c., &c.

Which for Beauty of Designs, Brilliancy of Colors and Durability, cannot be excelled by any establishment in the Union.

Hotels, Churches, Steamboats, Lodge Rooms, Public and Private Buildings, furnished at the most reasonable Prices.

Merchants, House-keepers, and all who contemplate furnishing, will find it to their interest to call and examine the assortment and prices before purchasing elsewhere.

Remember, No. 25 South Second St.

Corner of Black Horse Alley.

S. C. FOULK,

LOAG, THE PRINTER, SANSOM ST HALL.

p
dol. e cantabile.
p
p
p
Cantabile con molto portamento.
pp
ff
sur le Theatre

MUSICAL BOXES

In richly ornamented Cases, playing beautiful Home Melodies, as well as choice Selections from the various Operas, including such Favorites as

"THE LAST ROSE OF SUMMER,"
"HOME! SWEET HOME,"
"ROBIN ADAIR,"
"THE MONASTERY BELLS,"
"LISTEN TO THE MOCKING BIRD,"
"AULD LANG SYNE,"
"ROCK ME TO SLEEP, MOTHER," &c., &c.

Also,

"CASTA DIVA,"	Norma.
"ROBERT TOI QUE J'AIME," . .	Robert le Diable.
"LIBIAMO,"	Traviata.
"QUE J'AIME LES MILITAIRES,"	Grand Duchesse de Gerolstein.
"AH NON GIUNGE,"	Somnambula.
"MISERERE," . . .	Trovatore, &c., &c.

We are enabled, as the result of personal attention in Europe, to offer the finest quality of Musical Boxes at very reasonable prices, they being made to our own order, of the best materials and workmanship, and the music selected by ourselves.

Can be forwarded safely by Express to any address.

FARR & BROTHER,

IMPORTERS OF

Watches, Jewelry, Silver Ware, Musical Boxes, &c.

No. 324 Chestnut Street, below Fourth,

PHILADELPHIA.

HOUSE ESTABLISHED 45 YEARS.

LOAG, THE PRINTER, SANSOM ST. HALL.

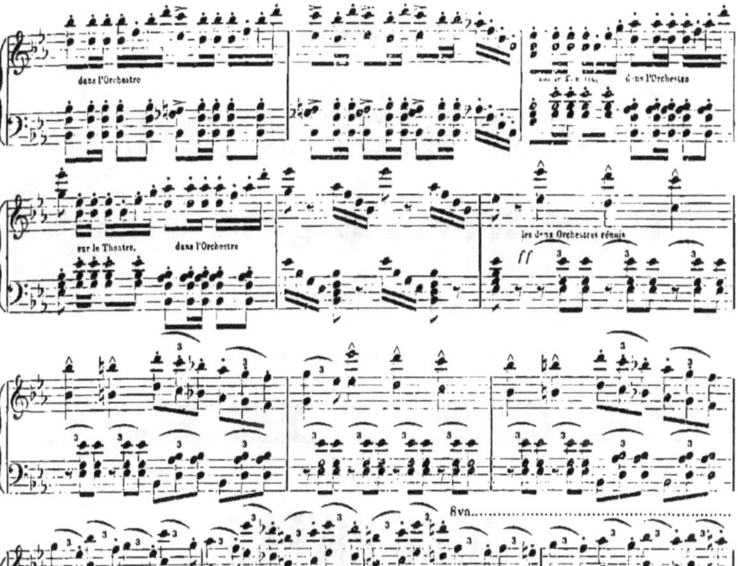

Published by Jules Bert.

J. W. HOFMANN,

No. 9 North Eighth Street,

PHILADELPHIA,

Offers for Sale a large assortment of

HOSIERY

AND

UNDERWEAR,

For Ladies, Gents, and Children.

Goods of medium and fine qualities, including the celebrated make of

CARTWRIGHT & WARNERS,

which are received direct from the manufacturers, and are recommended for durability and unshrinking qualities.

N. B.—A good assortment of Hosiery and Underwear, suited to any climate, on hand all the year round.

Established in 1848.

FANTASIE ON AIRS
FROM
DON CARLOS.

Hugh A. Clarke.

THE

FLORENCE

Makes Four different Stitches.

LOCK STITCH.   DOUBLE LOCK STITCH.   DOUBLE KNOT STITCH.   KNOT STITCH.

SEWING MACHINE

Is the best for Family use, combining

STRENGTH, BEAUTY, DURABILITY AND SIMPLICITY.

It stands without a Rival, having taken the Highest Premiums

AT THE

Pennsylvania State Fair, 1863; Mechanics' Institute, San Francisco, 1864; American Institute, Gold Medal, New York, 1865; State Fairs, California, 1865 and 1866; Paris Exposition, 1867; New England Agricultural Fair, Providence, R. I., 1867; New York State Fair, Buffalo, N. Y., 1867; Mechanics' Association, Lowell, Mass., 1867; Maryland Institute, Baltimore, Md., 1867; American Institute, New York, 1867. And also at every County Fair, where true merit and *Samples of Work made on the Machine* were the test.

We warrant every machine to be all that we claim for it, and will give a written warranty if required. We invite special attention to some of the great improvements over other machines, united in the FLORENCE SEWING MACHINE:

It is the only machine that makes four kinds of stitch, three of which are made on no other machine, and are stronger and more elastic than any other. It is the only Machine that can sew in more than one direction, having a reversible feed. It is the only Machine having a self-adjusting tension in shuttle—a great improvement. It fastens the ends of its seams better and quicker than a seamstress can. It uses less thread than any other machine. It runs light and quiet. It can be easily managed by a child. It needs only to be seen to satisfy any one of its superiority over all others. The "FLORENCE" will sew everything needed in a family, from the heaviest to the lightest fabric. It has a better hemmer than any other, and easier to manage. It hems, fells, cords, braids, tucks, quilts, gathers, &c., without basting. It makes a gather and sews it to a band at one operation, perfectly. It does more work, and more kinds of work than any other machine. It has a complete set of tools and fixtures.

A full assortment of Machines and Findings, with Samples of Work, at the Rooms of the Company.

1123 Chestnut Street, Phila., Pa.

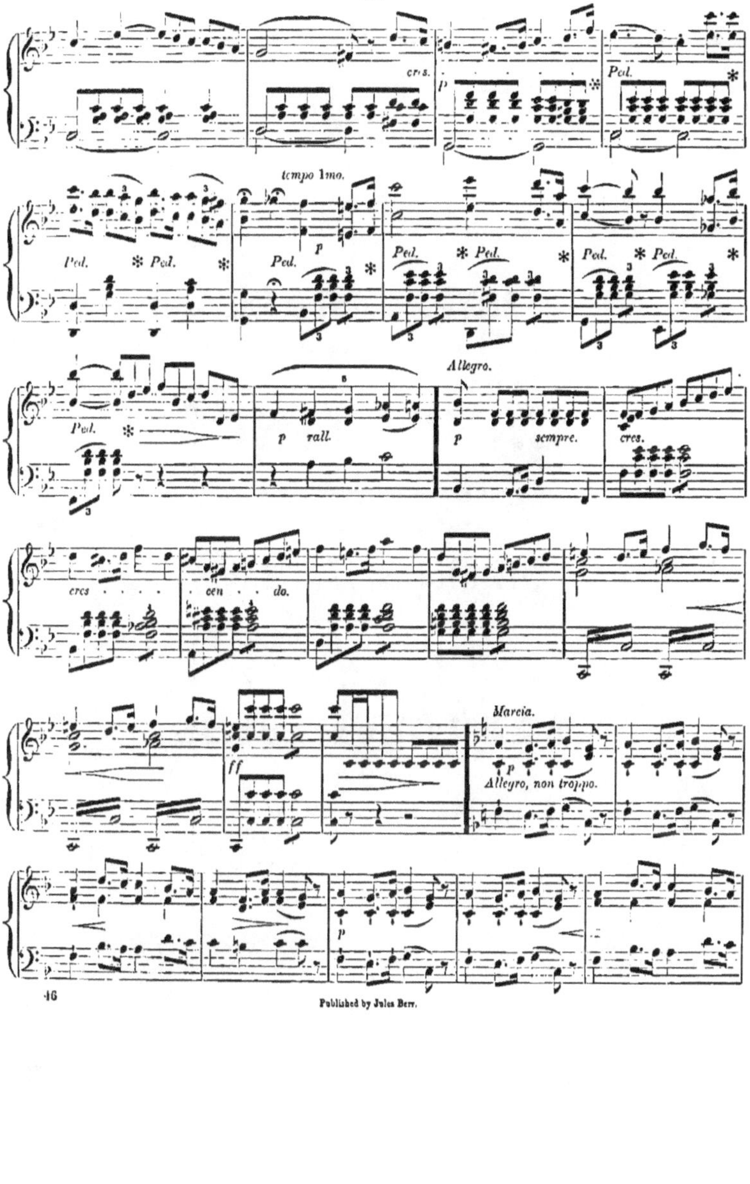

Published by Jules Berr.

REEVE L. KNIGHT & SON,

Importers and Dealers

IN

CARPETINGS

OF ALL DESCRIPTIONS.

Oil Cloths, Mattings, Druggets, &c.

1222 Chestnut St.

ABOVE TWELFTH.

PHILADELPHIA.

LOAG, THE PRINTER, SANSOM ST. HALL.

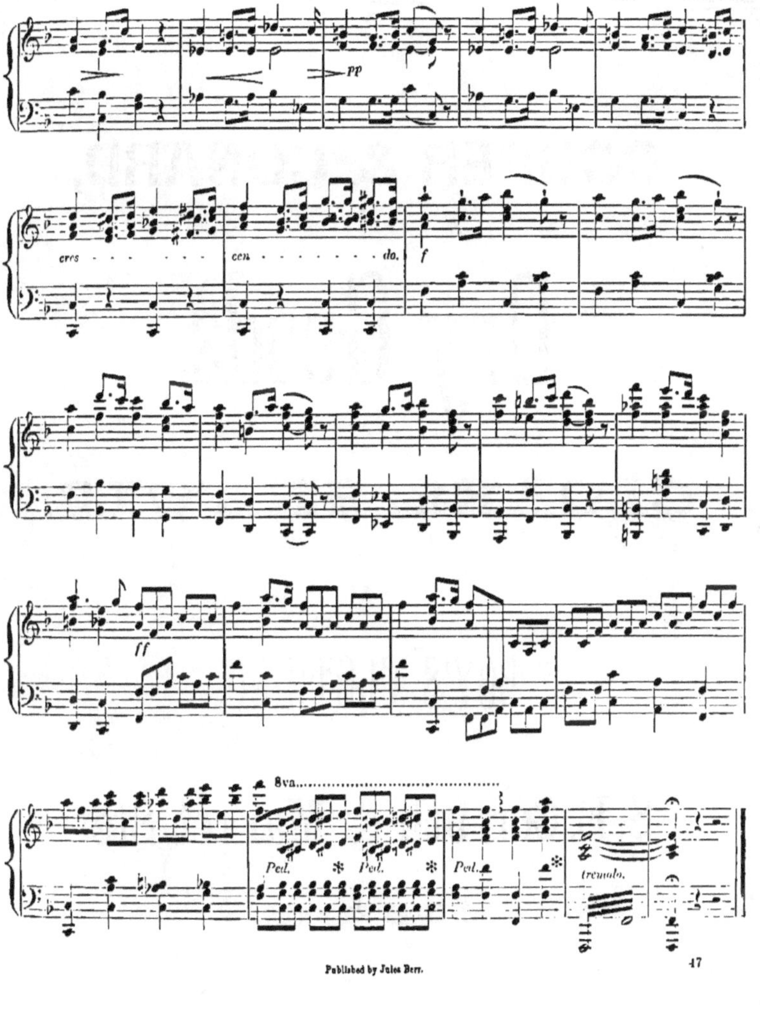
pp
cres - - - - - - - cen - - - - - - - - - - do.
f
ff
8va
Ped.
Ped.
Ped.
tremolo.

COOPER & CONARD,

Dry Goods,

CLOAKS, SHAWLS,

AND

BOY'S CLOTHING,

S. E. Cor. 9th & Market Sts.

PHILADELPHIA.

LOAG, THE PRINTER, SANSOM ST. HALL.

LA GRANDE DUCHESSE DE GEROLSTEIN.

OPÉRA DE
J. OFFENBACH.

QUADRILLE PAR
H. MARX.

Published by Jules Burr.

Nº. 3. POULE.

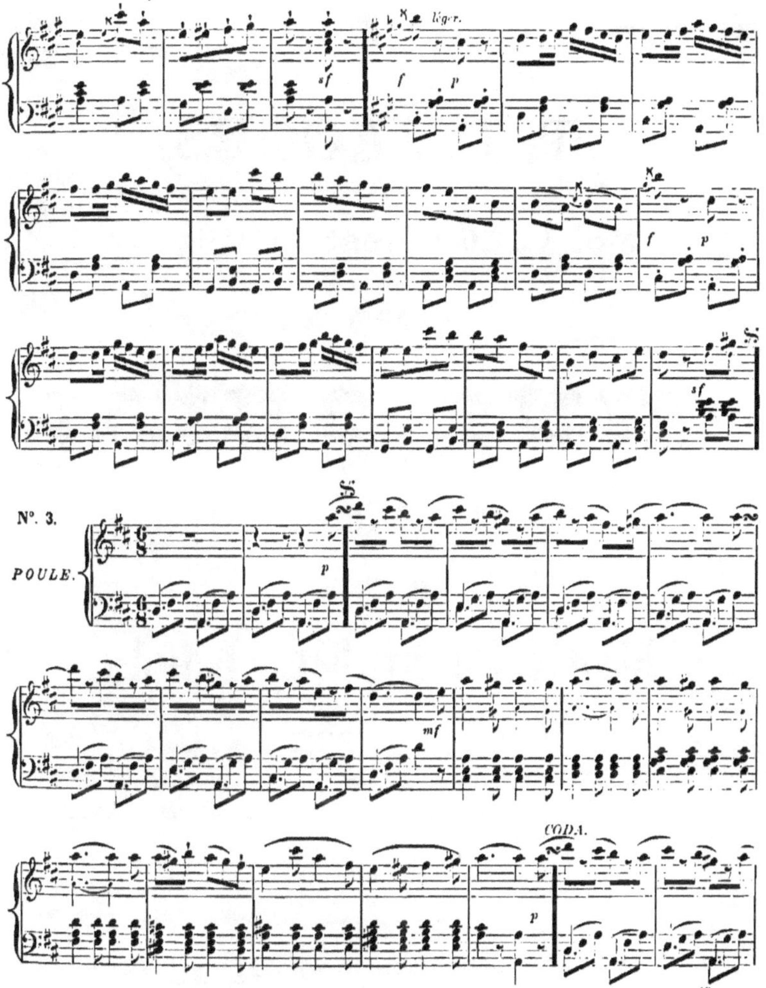

T. L. JACOBS,

No. 1226 Chestnut Street,

PHILADELPHIA,

FINE SHIRT

MANUFACTURER,

AND DEALER IN

Men's Furnishing Goods.

*I use in all Ordered Work the best makes of Richardson's Linen.
Money refunded if not satisfactory. I would call the attention
of the Ladies to my superior make of Boy's Shirts.
All Goods sold at the lowest possible prices.*

A LIBERAL DEDUCTION TO WHOLESALE TRADE.

N°. 4.

PASTOURELLE.

Published by Jules Berr.

Assorted Bon-Bons,   Chrystalized Fruits.

HAINES & LEEDS,
WHOLESALE & RETAIL

MANUFACTURERS OF

CHOICE

FINE CONFECTIONS

No. 906

Market Street, Phila.

Fruits, Nuts, &c.

Superfine Chocolate.   Superfine Almonds.

LOAG, THE PRINTER, SANSOM ST. HALL.

N°. 5.

FINALE.

2°. et 4°. Fois.

léger.

THE GUARDS' WALTZ.

D. GODFREY.

Andante.

INTRODUCTION.

Tempo di Valse.

Published by Jules Bore.

CONRAD BROTHERS,
1107
Chestnut Street, (Girard Row,)

MANUFACTURERS OF

SHIRTS

AND

MEN'S FURNISHING GOODS

IMPORTERS OF AND DEALERS IN

Fancy & Toilet Articles,

FINE FRENCH PERFUMERY & KID GLOVES.

Most careful attention given and satisfaction
guaranteed.

PRICES FAIR.

1107 Chestnut Street, Philad'a.

No. 1.

WALTZ

Published by Jules Barr.

Published by Jules Bora.

Special to the Ladies.

BOYS' CLOTHING

DEPARTMENT

ALL ON OUR

FIRST FLOOR,

Wanamaker & Brown,

The Largest Clothing House,

S. E. COR. SIXTH & MARKET STS.

PHILADELPHIA.

NOTE.—We not only save our lady friends the trouble of going up-stairs, but save them much time in selecting and fitting, as we have re-organized our Boys' Department, and will henceforth always have the largest assortment and most reasonable prices in the city.

LOAG, THE PRINTER, SANSOM ST. HALL.

3.

DREKA,

Importing Stationer

CARD ENGRAVER & PLATE PRINTER,

In all their various Branches.

American, French and English Stationery

OF THE FIRST QUALITY.

New Styles received and introduced as soon as issued in
Paris and London.

Arms, Crests, Monograms and Cyphers

Designed, Engraved and Illuminated in proper colors.

Particular attention given to

WEDDING AND VISITING CARDS,

Which are prepared in the most approved style, of the best materials
and workmanship.

All Designing, Engraving, Illuminating, Stamping and Card Printing executed in the
establishment by first-class artists, under the personal superintendence of Mr. Dreka.

Also, on hand, a very fine and constantly renewed assortment of neat and artistic
FANCY ARTICLES in the Stationery line, of American, French, English and German
manufacture.

GOODS IMPORTED TO ORDER.

LOUIS DREKA,

No. 1033 CHESTNUT STREET, PHILADELPHIA.

Published by Jules Berr.

WILLIAMS & WOODWARD

PROPRIETORS OF

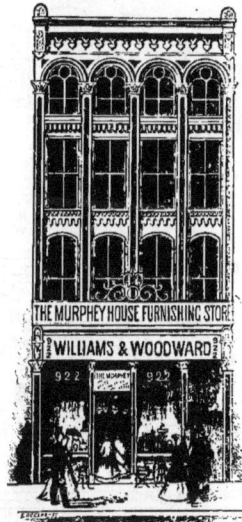

THE MURPHEY HOUSE FURNISHING STORE

WILLIAMS & WOODWARD

922   922

Coal Vase.
For keeping coal in parlors.

"THE MURPHEY"

HOUSE FURNISHING STORE,

No. 922 (Nine Twenty-two) Chestnut St.

PHILADELPHIA.

LOAG, THE PRINTER, SANSOM ST. HALL.

LA TRAVIATA.

By Verdi.

Arr. by H. Cramer.

Allegretto. (BRINDISI nell'INTRODUZIONE: Libiamo ne' lieti calici.)
con grazia. leggerissino.

Largo. (FINALE II: Vole a fuggir la.) 8va..........

J. C. McCURDY & CO.

No. 140 North Eighth St., Philadelphia,

(Late McCurdy, Dunkle & Co.)

Dress Goods,

Black Silks, Silks in Colors,

MOURNING GOODS,

House Furnishing Goods, White Goods,

Corsets, Hoop Skirts, Hosiery and Gloves,

AT LOW PRICES.

No. 140 North Eighth Street

PHILADELPHIA.

LOAG, THE PRINTER, SANSOM ST. HALL.

8va......................

Allo. brillante. (ARIA: Sempre libera.)

Published by Jules Berr.

HAMRICK & COLE,

WHITE MARBLE BUILDING,

No. 45 North Eighth Street,

IMPORTERS, JOBBERS AND RETAILERS OF

DRY GOODS,

Silks, Velvets,

HOUSEKEEPING GOODS,

NOTIONS, &c., &c.

ALWAYS AT POPULAR PRICES,

LOAG, THE PRINTER, SANSOM ST. HALL.

Andantino. (SCENA ed ARIA: Ah forse è lui che l'anima.)

con espress.

128

Andante, più tosto mosso. (SCENA ed ARIA: Di Provenza il mar.)

Published by Jules Dett.

IL TROVATORE.

(Canzone: *Stride la vampa.*)

VERDI.

Published by Jules Bece.

61

Andante mosso. (*Terzetto: Qual per esso provo amore.*)

Allo. agitato. (*Aria: Tu vedrai che amore.*)
sotto voce.

62

Published by Jules Borr.

J. W. PROCTOR & CO.

IMPORTERS, JOBBERS & RETAILERS

OF

FOREIGN AND DOMESTIC

DRY GOODS,

Black and Colored Silks,
Plain and Fancy Dress Goods,
Cloaks, Mantillas and Shawls,
Laces and Embroideries,
Hosiery and Gloves,
Cloak & Dress Trimmings
and Ornaments,

White Goods, Linens and Domestics,

No. 920 CHESTNUT STREET,

PHILADELPHIA.

J. W. PROCTOR.   DAVID HUGHES.

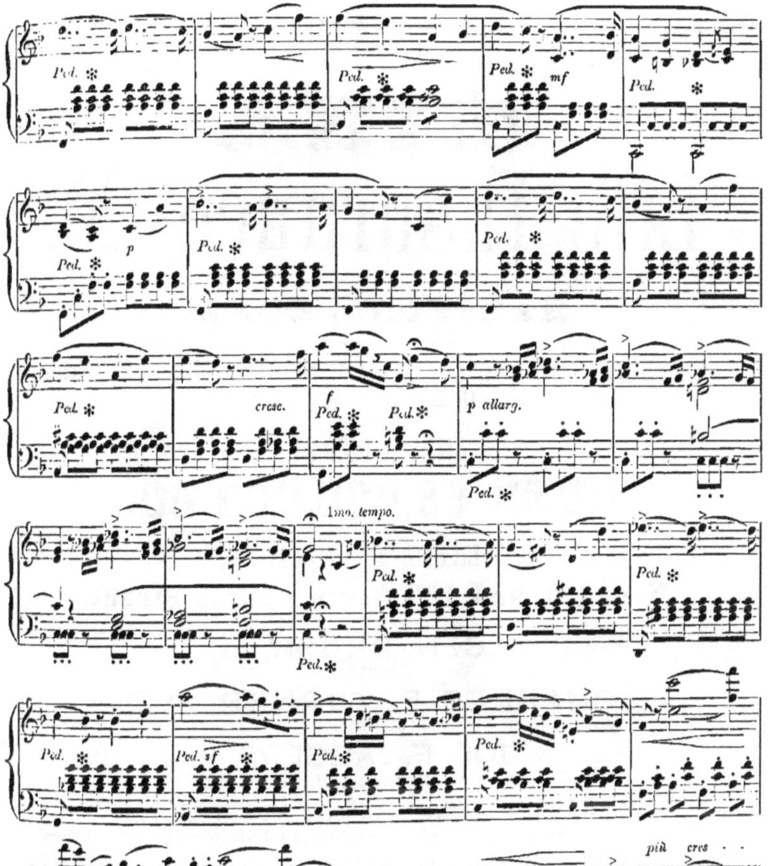

Published by Jules Bert.

Published by Jules Birr.

Jouvin's Kid Gloves, Embroideries & Lace Goods.

DAILY RECEIVING NEW GOODS.

E. R. LEE,

DRY GOODS

No. 43

North Eighth Street,

PHILADELPHIA.

LOAG, THE PRINTER, SANSOM ST. HALL.

137

GRANDE DUCHESSE DE GEROLSTEIN.

IT IS A LEGEND OLD.

(LEGENDE DU VERRE.)

J. OFFENBACH.

Allegro. (♩ = 100)
G. Duchesse.

VOICE.

1. It is a legend old I tell, What in my father's days be - fel, Of
1. Il é - tait un de mes aï - eux Le-quel si j'ai bon - ne mé - moi - re Se
2. One day, while full of wine and mirth, He let it fall up - on the earth, The
2. Un jour, on ne sait pas comment, Il le lais - sa tom - ber par ter - re, Ah!

PIANO.

p

Solo or Chorus
ad lib.

one in drink - ing fa - mous quite, Who'd leave the moderns out of sight. . . . Of
vau - tait d'être un des fa - meux Par - mi les gens qui savaient boi - - re. Se
earth, not fond of wine, a - las! Broke all to splin - ters this gay glass. . . The
dit - il dou - lou - reu - se - ment Vo - là que j'ai cas - sé mon ver - - re. Ah!

f

Published by Jules Berr.

65

G. Duchesse.

one in drink - ing fa - mous quite, Would leave the mo - derns out of
van - tait d'être un des fa - meux l'ar - mi les gens qui sa - vaient
earth, not fond of wine, a - las! Broke all to splin - ters this gay
dit - - il dou - lou - reu - se - ment Voi - là que j'ai cas - sé mon

sight. The glass in which he drank would hold Just a cask full, I am told . . There-
boi - re Le ver - re qu'il a - vait te - nait Un peu plus qu'une tonne en - tiè - re Et
glass. And when they wish'd to make a new, No, said he, that will nev - er do. . . I'd
verre Quand on vou - lut le rem-pla - cer Non dit - il ce n'est pas le no - tre Et

Solo or Chorus
ad lib.

- in his ser - vants day and night Pour'd wine; he drank all with de - light. . . There-
son é - chan - son lui ver - sait Nuit et jour du vin dans ce ver - re Et
ra - ther nev - er drink at all Then touch an - oth - er great or small. . . I'd
mieux il ai - ma tré - pas - ser Que boi - re ja - mais dans un au - tre Et

Published by Jules D...

LANCASTER'S

INSURANCE AGENCY,

N. W. Cor. Fourth & Walnut Streets.

CAPITAL,

$13,000,000.

COMPANIES REPRESENTED.

LORILLARD, NEW YORK,	$1,500,000	EXCELSIOR, NEW YORK,	410,000
FULTON, NEW YORK,	410,000	MERCANTILE, NEW YORK,	295,000
RELIEF, NEW YORK,	300,000	HOWARD, BALTIMORE,	250,000
RESOLUTE, NEW YORK,	295,000	N. Y. ACCIDENTAL INS. CO.	300,000

NEW YORK LIFE INSURANCE COMPANY,
Cash Assets, $10,000,000.

DIVIDENDS.

The business of this Company is STRICTLY MUTUAL, all the surplus being divided annually among the members, in cash, or the dividends can be applied to increase the sum assured, and at any subsequent period to assist in the payment of premiums.

Policies Issued on Household Furniture for Five Years at a reduced rate of Premium.

FIRE, LIFE, MARINE, INLAND, and ACCIDENTAL INSURANCE
PLACED TO ANY AMOUNT BY

THOMAS J. LANCASTER,
N. W. Cor. Fourth & Walnut Sts.
PHILADELPHIA.

- in   his   ser - vants   day   and   night Pour'd wine; he   drank   all   with   de-
son   é - chan - son   lui   ver - sait Nuit et   jour   du   vin   dans   ce
ra - ther nev - er   drink   at   all, Than touch an - oth - er,   great   or
mieux   il   ai - ma   tré - pas - ser Que boi - re   ja - mais   dans   un

O. Duchess.

- light.   What   a   to - per,   and what   wine!   Ah! . . .   Ah!
ver - - re,   du   vin!   du   vin!   Ah! . . .   Ah!
small, . . . an - oth - er   great or   small.   Ah! . . .   Ah!
au - - tre,   Que   boi - re   dans un   au - tre.   Ah! . . .   Ah!

ff

grandsire,   what   a   to - per you,   And what   a   migh - ty   glass   to   view. Ah!
mon   aï - eul comme il   bu - vait   Et   quel grand verre il   vous   a - vait. Ah!

pp

H. STEEL & SON,

HAVE ALWAYS ON HAND A

LARGE ASSORTMENT OF

Silks, Shawls,

AND

FINE DRESS GOODS,

EMBRACING ALL THE

Latest Foreign Novelties,

WHITE GOODS,

GLOVES AND HOSIERY,

CLOAKING CLOTHS,

And a large Stock of every variety of

DOMESTIC DRY GOODS,

Nos. 713 & 715 N. Tenth St.

PHILADELPHIA.

LOAG, THE PRINTER, SANSOM ST. HALL.

what a glass, Ah! what a glass, Ah! what a glass, a glass to view. Ah! . . . .
quel grand verre, Ah! quel grand verre, Ah! quel grand verre il vous a - vait. Ah! . . . .

. . . and what a migh - ty glass had you, Ah! what a migh - ty
. . . Et quel grand verre il vous a - vait, Ah! quel grand verre on

glass had you, had you, . . . had you!
vous a - vait il vous . . . a - vait!

8va............

Published by Jules Berr.

ARIA FROM ROMEO ET JULIETTE.

Arr. by H. A. CLARKE.

Entered according to Act of Congress, in the year 1865, by JULES BEBE, in the Clerk's office of the District Court for the Eastern District of Pennsylvania.

DEDICATED TO EPSTEIN & HAINES.

Published by Jules Berr.

W. & J. AKERS,

Importers and Dealers in

FRENCH CHINA, GLASS

AND

QUEENSWARE,

Table Cutlery, Silver Plated Goods,

TEA TRAYS, &c.

No. 823 Market St.

Above Eighth,

PHILADELPHIA.

Published by Jules Berr.

HOUSEKEEPER'S
FURNISHING STORE

ESTABLISHED, 1804.

ISAAC S. WILLIAMS & CO.

No. 728 Market Street,

PHILADELPHIA,

Where may be found, of the best quality, and for sale at fair prices, a full assortment of

HOUSEKEEPING HARDWARE,

Table and Kitchen Cutlery,

Tin and Japanned Ware, Plated and Britannia Goods, Brushes, Brooms,
Baskets, Wooden Ware,

REFRIGERATORS,

Wire Covers, Chamois Skins, and all the variety of articles in the line
required for furnishing a house.

LOAG, THE PRINTER, SANSOM ST. HALL.

BOHEMIAN GIRL.

DE BALFE.

DIE ZIGEUNERIN.

H. CRAMER.

Allegretto. (Romanze mit Chorus: Folgt der Zigeunerbraut.)

Published by Jules Berr.

Published by Jules Bern.

73

155

74

Published by John Barr.

CHAMPAGNE CHARLIE.

Written by GEORGE LEYBOURNE.

Music by ALFRED LEE.

1. I've seen a deal of gay-e-ty through-out my noi-sy life, With
2. The way I gain'd my ti-tles by a hob-by which I've got, Of

all my grand ac-complish-ments I ne'er could get a wife, The
ne-ver let-ting o-thers pay, how-e-ver long the shot, Who-

J. A. YOST,

MANUFACTURER OF

CHILDREN'S CARRIAGES,

Perambulators, Hobby Horses,

PROPELLERS, WHEEL-BARROWS,

WAGONS, CARTS, &c.

Manufactory, Cor. Third St. and Girard Av.

STORE,

49 North 9th Street,

NEAR ARCH,

PHILADELPHIA.

thing I most ex - - cel in is the P. R. F. G. game, A
ev - er drinks at my ex - pense are treat - ed all the same; From

noise all night, in bed all day, and swim - ming in Cham - pagne. For
Dukes and Lords to Cab - men down, I make them drink Cham - pagne. For

Chorus.

Champagne Char - lie is my name, . . . Cham - pagne Char - lie is my name, . . .

Good for an - y game at night, my boys, good for an - y game at night, my boys,

Published by Jules Berr.

WILLIAM W. ALTER,

DEALER IN

BEST QUALITIES OF

COAL

Yard and Office,

957 North Ninth St. 957

BELOW GIRARD AVENUE.

Branch Office, 6th & Spring Garden Sts.

Orders by Mail promptly attended to.

Champagne Char-lie is my name. . . . Cham-pagne Char-lie is my name, . . .

Good for an-y game at night, boys, who'll come and join me in a spree.

3. From coffee and from supper-rooms, from Poplar to Pall Mall,
The girls on seeing me exclaim, "Oh! what a Champagne swell!"
The notion 'tis of every one, if 'twere not for my name,
And causing so much to be drunk, they'd never make Champagne.
  Cho.—For Champagne Charlie, &c.

4. Some epicures like Burgundy, Hock, Claret, and Moselle,
But Moet's Vintage only satisfies this Champagne swell;
What matter if to bed I go, and head is muddled thick,
A bottle in the morning sets me right then very quick.
  Cho.—For Champagne Charlie, &c.

5. Perhaps you fancy what I say is nothing else but chaff,
And only done, like other songs, to merely raise a laugh;
To prove that I am not in jest each man a bottle of Cham-
I'll stand fizz round—yes that I will, and stand it—like a lamb.
  Cho.—For Champagne Charlie, &c.